Facebook Marketing

A Comprehensive Guide to Growing

Your Business on Facebook

Jason Lazar

Table of Contents

Introduction 1

Chapter 1: Growing Your Business on Facebook 3

Chapter 2: Facebook Marketing Strategies 13

Chapter 3: Content Creation 23

Chapter 4: Facebook Marketing Structure 29

Chapter 5: How to Set Up Facebook Ad Sets 46

Chapter 6: Running Facebook Ads 56

Chapter 7: Managing Your Ads 66

Chapter 8: Remarketing and Retargeting 74

Conclusion 84

Introduction

Facebook is one of the largest social networks with millions of daily users. Many businesses have embraced social media marketing, with an understanding of how beneficial it can be on sales and profits. On the other hand, some businesses look at it as a waste of time or too small of a factor to take seriously. But if you could easily promote your business, products, and services for free in front of your target audience, wouldn't you want to take advantage of that?

Most businesses approach Facebook with the idea that they need to spend significant amounts of money to see any substantial returns. This thinking is why many businesses fail to capitalize on the huge untapped market in front of them. Without basic understanding or embracing the social aspect of the platform, businesses waste time and money, and eventually abandon the whole process.

If you have tried to get your business noticed on Facebook but have struggled to grow your following, there's a good chance you are not doing the basic steps that will yield the result you are eager to see. Without the basic steps, you have no foundation to build a solid ad campaign around. Where most businesses fail is, they try to use the same marketing strategies from other avenues on Facebook and hope for the same results. Even trying to copy your marketing strategy from another social platform won't get you the results you want. You need to fully understand how to stand out and get noticed.

Building your business on Facebook requires a new strategy, new objectives, and a new perspective. In this book, you will learn how to optimize your marketing strategy from beginning to end. First, you will learn how to set up a business page that will get you more views, and a higher ranking in news feeds. Then you will learn how to create a clear vision of your end goal. You will learn there is much more to gain from a strong Facebook presence than just a few extra sales. You will learn the most important component of your Facebook marketing strategy (and it isn't running ads). The last half of this book provides you with an in-depth look at how to run ads. You will learn the formats, types, and best ways to optimize Facebook ads to move towards your marketing goals.

Millions of companies already know the powerful impact of a successful Facebook marketing strategy, and they are taking advantage of it. Your business and brand should be one of those millions, and with the help of this book, it can be!

Chapter 1: Growing Your Business on Facebook

If you aren't taking advantage of Facebook to grow your business, you are missing out and letting competition pass you by. With over 2.6 billion users and over 1.7 billion people using it daily, there is a huge pool of people your business could be getting in front of. Why are more businesses not taking advantage of this platform? If you don't think your business will benefit from Facebook, you will begin to change your perspective once you understand its potential.

Leveraging Facebook to Grow Your Business

Facebook is a social platform, which means the whole purpose of this site is to connect with friends and family. There is a large pool of users who log on to stay connected to their favorite brands as well. Businesses can use this to connect people with their brand, products, and services. The approach you take to using Facebook to grow your business will differ from other businesses, as it should. The most successful businesses have been able to stand out because they take advantage of all the tools and features Facebook offers to make an impact.

Should Your Business Be on Facebook?

Small business owners should certainly be taking advantage of all Facebook has to offer. Those looking into influencer marketing should also be utilizing Facebook to strengthen their personal brand. Solopreneurs, artists, online merchants, service providers, and nearly any other type of business, big or small, should be on Facebook to either extend reach, grow their business, or branch out into other areas. Businesses that use Facebook effectively to grow their business have seen an increase in sales, improvement in customer service, customer loyalty, and many other benefits.

Not only does Facebook provide you with an easy to navigate platform, but it also allows you to find followers and for more fans to easily find you. It is one of the most visited sites and is one that people spend the most time on. Despite its high user rate, it is a low-cost marketing option for small businesses, and one even those starting out can afford. Most marketing done on Facebook costs nothing at all, only when you want to maximize your efforts will you need to invest a little more.

Reasons Why Businesses Fail on Facebook

While Facebook can easily bring more eyes to your business, most fail to capitalize on the opportunity to grow. The number one reason isn't that business owners don't understand how to use the platform, more often than not, page owners aren't clear about their goals or effort needed to be put into continuously growing and maintaining a fanbase.

They don't utilize all the features Facebook has to offer. There is a lot you can do on Facebook aside from creating a page and asking friends to like and follow you. Setting up pages, groups, events, and running ads are just a few of the other ways you can expand your reach on Facebook.

They don't take engagement seriously enough. Businesses that add a human touch to their engagement and posting will lead to more people being interested in what you and your business have to say. Remember, Facebook at its core is a social network. To be social you need to add a human tone, interest, and elements throughout your page and in all interactions.

They aren't consistent, which unfortunately means they aren't standing out. To gain attention on Facebook you need to be posting regularly, only posting a few times a month or even once a week means your outreach isn't being seen. Inconsistent posts get lost in the crowd of the many other people and businesses who update daily.

They are not adding value by entertaining, educating, or exciting their audiences. Most people on Facebook are there for entertainment. They just want to waste time or have a good laugh. Once you captivate your audience in an entertaining way, you need to add value through education. Intriguing an audience gives them a reason to want to check in often. They are interested in what you will post next and are more likely to click on the links you share.

Profile Page vs Business Page

Profile or page, which do you need for your business? The main difference is a page is dedicated specifically for businesses. If you have a business and are relying on a Facebook profile to grow, you are going about marketing on Facebook the wrong way.

A page provides more than a standard profile. First, you get additional marketing tools and in-depth data when you run a page. This helps you see how your business is growing, and how much traction your efforts are making. Another reason to set up a page is to gather reviews. This will often lead to those less familiar with you deciding if they want to give your business or service a try.

You can set up a separate account and create a profile for your business as if it were an actual person, but you won't get the perks of a page. You need to have a profile linked to the page, which you can do using your personal profile or by setting up a business profile.

How to Set up a Page

This process is fairly similar to setting up a standard profile page. Before you create your page, do a quick search of the name you plan to use for your business. You want the name to be unique to ensure your business does not get confused with another page or profile that may have similar spelling. After you have done a quick search and are certain about the name you want to display, choose the Create Page options from the left side panel of your profile page. From here you will enter in the business name as opposed to your own name and add a description in the About section. Like a profile, you will want to add business details and a relevant cover photo.

To create a separate business account, you will need to go to the web address business.Facebook.com/create. From here you will be prompted to sign into your account to verify your credentials. On this page, you will find the steps necessary for setting up everything you need to manage and expand your business on Facebook.

Optimizing Your Page

Optimizing your business page ensures the most eyes get directed towards you. This is crucial for when you begin to set up ads. It doesn't take a great deal of extra time to optimize your page, but most businesses fail to do so.

Include All Information

There is plenty of information you can include on your page and you never want to leave anything blank. Facebook favors businesses that have all their 'About' information entered. Location is an essential area to fill in. Even if you work from home, set your location to the closest city. This will help other users find your business and help Facebook know who to show your posts and ads to. Adding a location establishes your business as legitimate and provides followers with comfort in knowing you are a trusted business.

Other information you want to add is:

- Full address (if you have a physical storefront)
- Phone number (for either texts or calls)
- Email
- Website
- Hours of operation

You also want to provide a description. This can be a brief story of your business, its purpose, products, and whatever you feel is important to note so that people viewing your page will be inclined to follow you.

Facebook Tabs

Facebook tabs are highly underused. Tabs help you keep your page organized and provide extra customized navigation to better serve your audience. You will notice tabs are already a part of your business page. They are located just below the cover photo, and along the left side panel. By default, these tabs include Timeline, About, Photos, Reviews, and a More tab. You can change and customize these tabs to draw attention to key services, freebies, and other information about your business. If you have an upcoming event, you can create a tab to have visitors register; if you have a guide or pamphlet you want your visitor to enjoy, make a tab for it. You can also make a tab to get to visitors to subscribe to your blog or mailing list.

CTA Button

The call-to-action (CTA) button is displayed just below your cover image on the right side. This can be used to drive followers to a specific link, but it can also encourage followers or page visitors to perform various actions. Some ways to use this feature include:

- Shop online store

- Book an appointment
- Make a donation
- Contact us

This button can remove additional steps your followers would typically have to perform like finding the link to your website to get contact information. It also makes it convenient for them to find a link to access your products or services. The more convenient it is for followers to see what you offer, the more likely they are to interact.

Personal URL

A typical Facebook URL consists of random numbers and letters, but you can create a more personalized URL with your business account. This can help more users find your business and provide them with an additional level of trust. It only takes a few extra minutes to set up.

To create your URL, you need to create a username. Go to your business page and find the Page@Username along the left side panel. Then type on the username you want to use; if it is available all you have to do is click Create Username. If the name you want is unavailable, you will need to come up with a different one. Capitalizing or adding periods in the username is prohibited. For instance, if you want to use legalname27 but it is taken, you will not be able to use LegalName27, Legal.Name.27, or any variation of this. Once you have created your username, your URL will automatically update to reflect the username you chose.

Keep in mind there are a few guidelines and regulations for creating your username. This includes only being able to use numbers and letters, and it must be at least five characters long. If your page remains inactive for too long your username can be revoked.

Pinned Posts

If you have a post that you want visitors to see first, you can pin it to the top of your news feed. Pinning posts is a great way to ensure that your followers don't forget about important information, or to remind them of an upcoming event or promotion. It can also be a way for you to let new visitors get to know you by pinning a welcome post that describes who you are and what your business is about. You can also do this with groups you create.

Groups and Communities

Groups are a great way to help build credibility and drive more traffic to your business. This is true whether you join an already established group or create one of your own. You can ask to join any number of groups and these can be directly related to your industry, product, or can be geared towards a specific demographic of those in your target audience, for example: moms over 30, or fitness fanatics.

These are tight-knit communities of individuals who all have common interests. Once you join a group you can easily begin to establish yourself as an expert on what current members are looking for. It is good practice to introduce yourself in any new group you are added to, just be sure to review the group rules and guidelines. Some groups will ban members for posting business or product ads unless specifically invited to do so. You can, however, display your credibility by answering questions, sharing helpful blog posts (even your own), or give suggestions for certain products (which can be something you sell or provide).

Groups are also a great place to find questions, concerns, and interests of your target audience. This will help you create content that will directly interest and attract those individuals to your business. It will also help you learn the language those in your target group use, which will allow you to set up your ads in a way that directly appeals to your audience.

Chapter 2: Facebook Marketing Strategies

As with any type of marketing you need to have a plan in place for it to be successful. After you have set up your business page, and ideally before you even publish it, you need to have a clear vision of what you want to achieve on this platform. Marketing on Facebook does not have to be overwhelming or complicated but if you do not establish a plan first, you will waste time, money, and miss out on opportunities.

Establishing Goals

Having a Facebook page will require time and attention. If you are not able to delegate your social media marketing to a hired professional, this is time you will need to put into growing your page. Whether you are taking on this responsibility or letting someone else do it for you, you need to have clear goals set to stay on track. It can be easy to get distracted and get caught in a cycle of constantly trying to reinvent your page for more engagement, but this will be wasted time and effort.

Setting goals from the beginning will provide you with what you want to measure. Are you trying to increase likes, build a mailing list, or strengthen your brand? You need to have clear goals to stay consistent and aligned with your purpose. Some goals you could set to do this include:

- Adding value through your content
- Increase your likes to at least 10,000
- Collect emails
- Monetize your page through different sources

Most of these goals will remain in place as your business continues to grow. You can set more specific terms and conditions for reaching them, then adjust along the way to match your growth (how many emails do you want to collect a week or month, how much income do you want to garner from additional sources each month, once you hit 10,000 likes what is the next milestone?).

Aside from the goals listed above, you will need to establish clear goals for your marketing and business. This gives you a clear path to building a community around your business. A successful social media goal will combine a business goal with a social platform goal. Your business goal can be to increase online sales, your social media goal in connection with this is to attract more customers to your store or website through posts.

When you want to create ads on Facebook you will need to select an objective. This objective should align with the long-term goals you have for your business and marketing plan. Not having goals already decided on will hold up this process or cause you to create ads that do not help you grow your business the way you hope.

How To Frame a Goal

The most effective way to create your social media business goals is through the SMART method:

- Specific
- Measurable
- Attainable
- Relevant
- Time-based

This framework lets you map out all the details to reach a desired outcome. You establish what it is that you will be able to measure, define a clear objective, and set a deadline for completion. These more specific goals will keep you motivated as you work towards a focused endpoint. When goals are too vague it is easier to set them aside or go in a different direction which results in wasted time and effort. SMART goals take the guesswork out of how to achieve your dream, while also establishing a timeframe for their completion.

Social media marketing goals need to focus on increasing conversion rates and building a solid brand. We will go deeper into the branding aspect in the next section. Conversion rate goals can be based on metrics such as:

1. Directing more traffic to your website.
2. Growing your email list.
3. Increasing sales for a set timeframe (Black Friday sales, end of Summer sales).

When you go to create your Facebook ads you will utilize a focus area like the three listed above to improve click-through rates, lower cost per click, and increase your relevancy score.

When we put all these factors together you will have a concrete goal to gauge your success. Some examples of clearly defined social media goals are:

- Increase website traffic to 3,000 visitors a month within the next three months before the next big product launch.
- Increase brand awareness by gaining 10,000 followers over the next 6 months with a focus on local reach to bring more foot traffic to the physical store.
- Increase blog traffic by 25% by the end of the year through paid and organic posts.
- Increase online sales by 30% before the holiday season by first increasing brand awareness and page engagement. Through remarketing ads, move current customers and newer followers through the funnel system.

Writing a Socials Mission Statement

Having a mission statement will make it easier to stick to goals and create a strong brand that people will rave about. You should already have a mission state established for your business outside of social media. It is also important to write a mission statement that directly connects to your social goals and how you want your business to be portrayed.

When you begin to create content for your business page you will quickly find that there is so much information you can share. The pressure to constantly post and share can lead to publishing things that don't align with the message you want the audience to receive from your business.

A mission statement will keep you on track, so your brand remains consistent. A few tips to keep in mind when you craft your Facebook mission statement:

1. Know what emotional connection your audience should feel when they see something from your business. Choose three core emotions you want to evoke when you put together a post.
2. Reflect your core object or goal for Facebook marketing.
3. Know what tone you want to use—knowledgeable, energetic, approachable, optimistic, etc.
4. Connect with your company's mission statement.

When writing your statement keep in mind what you want to be known for. When people visit your page what are the top three things that stand out? Do you want to encourage and empower your audience, inform and educate, or entertain and bring a smile to their face? Your mission statement should directly reflect what your audience expects when they see your posts. Before you post, run an ad, or leave a comment, revisit your mission statement. Ensure that what you are offering to your community aligns with this mission.

Branding

Most social media goals will strive to strengthen branding and achieve better conversion rates. Facebook is the ideal platform for strengthening your brand identity for your business or as an influencer. Brand awareness is one of the top reasons that businesses turn to Facebook to grow their business.

When you use Facebook to grow your business, you are essentially using it as a platform to bring more awareness to your brand. If you don't have an established brand, your efforts will seem scattered and mediocre at best. In the past, branding was simple and easily identified by a memorable logo and catchphrase or smart slogan. Now, however, a brand is a full entity that is humanized and relatable. Your brand is what people will connect with, it is what will make them want to engage with you and ultimately choose you over the thousands of other options.

Building a brand involves:

- Growing a community through likes and followers.
- Expand your reach by posting regularly.
- Encourage engagement through shareable content, responding to comments, and asking questions.
- Telling the story of your business.

Branding for Influencers

Influencer marketing has quickly become a crucial component for a business marketing strategy no matter what platform they use. Influencers looking to grow their own brand awareness on Facebook need to have a clear unique image that gets them noticed. Businesses need to improve their brand awareness to intrigue influencers to use and mention products or services on their profile page.

The key factors that influencers need to focus on to build brand awareness, and what a business needs to look for in an influencer include:

- **Loyal and large following**: The specific number of followers you want to have will vary depending on the company, but aside from the size, you want fans that are loyal. People need to be commenting, sharing, liking, and talking about what you post regularly.

- **Engaging content**: If you can create eye-catching content you are going to get noticed by multiple companies. The main reason companies choose to work with influencers is because they can get their followers to talk about products and keep them interested.

- **Be genuine**: Whether you give a certain product a rave review or your honest opinion, you need to be authentic. Businesses don't want to work with an influencer who is just going to say what they think they should say. They want to work with an influencer who is relatable.

Influencers looking to build their personal brand should follow the practices of other successful businesses on Facebook. You are your own business, and you need to treat your Facebook profile or page with the same professionalism that successful businesses treat their pages with.

Being Consistent

Consistency is crucial for growing your brand. The tone you use in your posts, the filters you use on your images, and the colors, fonts, and style of your images, texts, and graphics should all be consistent. This will help identify your brand and let your posts stand out in feeds. When a follower sees your post, they should automatically know what brand it came from.

You also have to be consistent with posting. You do not need to continuously share new content, but you do need to post on a regular schedule, such as once per day, to stay at the forefront of your audience's news feeds.

Understanding the Facebook Algorithm

Facebook is constantly changing its algorithm, but one thing remains consistent with each new change; they always focus on how relevant posts are. Instead of displaying content chronologically, they are always changing their algorithm so that the most relevant posts are seen first and more often. This takes several things into consideration.

- The highest-ranking posts are those from friends and family.

- Posts with high comments, likes, and shares often get top priority in most news feeds.
- Images and graphics are preferred over plain text posts.
- Getting a lot of likes, shares, and comments in a short time period.
- Posts that get shared by friends of followers.
- Posts that discuss trending topics.
- Linked posts.
- Post from pages that have all profile information filled out.
- Posts from pages that have an overlapping follower list similar to well-known higher-ranking pages.

Things the algorithm is not a fan of:

- Spam.
- Repeated posts.
- Click baiting.
- Pages that only post plain text content.
- Post that directly asks for likes, shares, or comments.
- Promotional posts that are too pushy asking for users to buy or use a specific product.

No matter what you discuss in your post or the type you share, the Facebook algorithm will work for you if you remain relevant.

Chapter 3: Content Creation

Creating content is the foundation for gathering valuable information on how to run successful Facebook ads. Most businesses focus on paid advertisement and neglect the content creation process. Before you can begin to run a successful ad campaign on Facebook, you need to give people a reason to stay connected. This can be done through your page posts.

Why Is Content So Important

Your content, or what you post, is what builds brand awareness. When done correctly it will build trust, let people see the human side of your business, and set you up as an expert in your industry. It is one of the easiest ways to communicate and engage with your audience. People are prone to buy from businesses they not only know, but also have a relationship with. Facebook helps you build that relationship through posts.

Posts can also help you reach a bigger audience without having to spend money on marketing. The average user on Facebook has around 200 friends. When one person shares your post, your business gets put in front of hundreds more people.

Your posts are what will keep your business relevant within the Facebook algorithm. If you are not posting regularly, this tells Facebook that you are not interested in the social aspect of their platform. People are looking for connection and valuable information; if you are not fostering both these needs, your business will not expand. If you only post once in a while, Facebook won't keep your posts in news feeds. Pages that post regularly and are engaged with will be visible on more news feeds.

Creating Content

When it comes to creating content to post, you want to narrow down your options. Instead of posting about a wide range of topics, stick to three to five key areas of focus. Users are not going to see every post you publish, and if you are posting about too many topics you are likely to lose your audience's attention. When you stick to a shorter list of topics you can stand out as the go-to place for information regarding these ideas.

Have a variety of posts that appeal to your audience. They can be:

- Text
- Images
- Video
- Live

- Linked posts
- Polls
- Stories

The type of post you publish should be based on your audience preferences. Most people will stop scrolling for images over plain text. Video, for example, is growing in popularity. Live streams tend to get more views than longer uploaded videos. Polls help increase engagement, and shared posts tend to provide the most value. When you begin posting you will want to pay particular attention to posts that get the most engagement.

After publishing on your business page, the best thing to do with your content is to find relevant ways to share it in groups. This is a great way to get your business out there without being pushy, spammy, or directly telling people to go to your site. Many groups look down on this, but if you posted something on your business page that helps answer a question in a group, share it.

One of the most underutilized forms of content is content you share from others. Along with that, it's important that you make your own content shareworthy. If one of your followers is willing to freely share your post on their own feed, that is valuable. This gets you ranked higher in the algorithm. While you don't necessarily want to directly ask followers to share, though many businesses do, you want to create content that makes an impact on your target audience. The more they relate to and connect with what you post, the more they will want to share.

Using the 70-20-10 Rule

Posting too many sales posts will get you penalized on Facebook. Not only will your sales post not get enough reach, but your other posts will be affected as well. Promotional posts, when not done correctly or done too often, cause users to block or hide posts from your page. Not only is this just bad for your marketing strategy, but Facebook also views this as irrelevant. Your posts will not be seen by as many people as they were before. When posting, it's good to follow the 70-20-10 rule to keep Facebook and your audience happy, but to also stay on track with your marketing goals.

This rule suggests that 70% of the content you post should be engaging and organic. These posts will help strengthen your brand identity and add value to your audience. The three to five core topics you chose to focus your content around will make up this 70% of content.

The 20% of your post should be shared. This means you are sharing posts from other pages and people that your audience would find interesting. Remember, shared posts get extra points in the Facebook algorithm. You still want this content to relate to your business, brand, or industry. You don't want to just post something with the hope of getting it shared.

The remaining 10% can be dedicated to self-promotion. These posts, however, still need to feel organic. While they may directly tell your followers to shop from your store, click on a link, or subscribe to your email list, you need to provide value and a good incentive for followers to take action. These posts need to be carefully related to all the other posts you have been pushing out during the week. If you are too spammy, followers will unfollow you, even if it is only once, and this will negatively impact your reach with future posts and ads.

Creating a Content Calendar

A content calendar will keep you consistent and your posts aligned with your mission statement. Tracking your content will also allow you to understand when your posts get the most engagement and what posts your audience prefers. You should already have key topic areas chosen for post ideas and know a general breakdown of what types of posts you should be sharing regularly. Your calendar will organize these key factors to relieve you from worrying about what to post next.

You don't have to complicate your calendar; it can be done in just a few steps:

1. If you haven't done so, use your three to five main topics to educate or add value to your customers.

2. Determine how many times you will post. You want this to be at least once a day for Facebook, but you can post more than that if you know your audience is likely to see what you are sharing.

3. Know what time of day to post. Posts shared between 9 am and 12 pm tend to get the most views, but there may be other peak times your target audience is on that you want to capitalize on. Knowing your audience will help you identify the best times to share posts and strategically post content that will appeal to them at that time. Wednesdays tend to be the highest activity days with the most users on Facebook.

Use apps like Buffer and Hootsuite to help you schedule posts and collect post ideas. Facebook also allows you to create posts and share them at a later time on your business page.

Chapter 4: Facebook Marketing Structure

Facebook ads are the smallest component of the overall marketing structure. This structure consists of the campaign, then ad sets, and finally the Facebook ad. Each of these tiers serves a specific purpose in the process. Understanding each component will guide you in creating your first Facebook ad.

Campaigns

Campaigns are where you will better organize your ads, and they are at the top tier of the Facebook marketing structure. These can contain multiple ad sets; properly naming and utilizing them can assist your marketing goals. When you name your campaign keep in mind it should be easy for you to identify the purpose of the ads here. Each campaign can have multiple ad sets, and single ads. You want each ad to align with the main objective of the campaign. Here are a few examples of working campaign names:

- Cold Marketing Campaigns
- Increase Website Traffic
- Build Brand Awareness
- Target Audience Women

- Lead Generating
- Product Promotions

You can make the campaign as detailed or as short as you prefer. When you create a new campaign, it will have an objective attribute. Each objective is organized into three main categories:

1. Awareness

There are two main objectives in this campaign category:

- Brand Awareness: This strengthens your brand awareness so that more people know about your business.
- Reach: When you first begin using Facebook for your business, your main objective will be to get as many people seeing your business as possible. With a reach objective, your ad will get shown to as many people in your target audience as possible.

2. Consideration

Consideration campaigns focus on driving traffic to their business to learn more about what they offer or provide. This category has the most options to choose from:

- Traffic: To increase traffic to a specific site via a URL, such as to your website or blog.

- Engagement: If your goal is to target people who will like, comment, and share your posts, this is the objective you will choose. This also includes targeting people who can claim an offer by going to your page, commenting, sharing, or tagging others.
- App installs: This objective is for those who want to create an ad that will drive more people to their store to download their business app.
- Video views: This objective is to get more people to watch videos put out by your business.
- Messages: This allows you to directly connect with people via messenger to increase interest in your business. These can be targeted to existing or potential customers.

3. Conversions

This type of campaign will focus on promoting your products or services to increase sales, or to get people to take a specific action. These goals may look similar to consideration goals with a key difference of getting people to use their products or service as opposed to just learning more about them. The objectives in this campaign category include:

- Conversions: These incorporate several actions. If your goal is to get more people to perform a specific task on your site such as add items to their cart, make a purchase,

or download an app, this is the objective you will want to use.
- Catalog sales: This object focuses on showing your products through your ad to get them to make a purchase.
- Store traffic: If your goal is to get more people to visit your physical location, you will need to set a store traffic objective.

Ad Sets

Ad sets are the next step in the process and are listed under specific ad campaigns. These sets are where you will determine how much you spend on your ads, your target audience, and scheduling. Each set will have multiple ads running that share similar settings. This is done so you can track which type of ad or format yields the best results in your target audience. By keeping certain attributes the same, you can test who responds more to your ads.

Typically, the target audience will change from one ad to another such as targeting men for one ad and women for another. The ad itself can remain identical. You just assign one copy to be targeted towards men, and another toward women. You may also like to test the market by changing the ad. You could, for example, use video in one and an image in another to see which your target audience responds to better. Gaining this knowledge of who is more likely to click on different types of ads will make your bidding more effective (more on that in the next chapter).

Ad sets can be general or specific. Some examples include:

- Ad set for men
- Ad set for women
- Ad set for people between 21 -30
- Ad set for people between 31-40
- Ad set for people 41-50
- Ad set for women 31-40
- Ad set for mothers 31-40

You can start by using a more general ad set to begin with, and then narrow down your target audience from there. The more specific you get with your ad set the better you can gauge and learn how to target your ads in the future.

Facebook Ads

Once you have your budget and audience in place, we move on to the ad creation. The ads will consist of images, videos, text, and links. You can use the same ad in different ad sets to see which audience they perform better in.

It is important to understand how to properly format each of the ad types within the guidelines Facebook has established for each. Your format will depend on the objects you choose, as some only allow for certain formats. For instance, if your adjective is to increase video views, you will need to use the video format. If you want to increase local awareness, you cannot use the canvas format.

Additionally, you can add text to any of your ads. First, you will add a brief tagline to the top of the image, not exceeding 90 characters. Next, you will create a heading for your ad. Headings are only visible on desktops and will appear below the image.

With each ad, you will have the ability to add a CTA button. For most, these include:

- Learn More
- Download
- Shop Now
- Sign Up
- Book Now
- Like Page
- Watch More

Different ads will have more options, but these are the standard for most. For increased video view ads, by default there is no CTA, but you can add one if you want. Let's go over the guidelines and what each type of ad creative entails:

Images

You can use your own images or choose from stock images. Some ads allow you to choose up to six different images so you can test which ones perform the best.

Guidelines:

- Images should be 1200X628 pixels with an image ratio of 8:3.
- If you are adding text to your images you want to ensure that no more than 20% of the image is text. In the past, ads were rejected when they exceeded this 20% rule; now they just do not get distributed as much and will cost more to run. It is good to keep this in mind as this leads to a more aesthetically pleasing ad and is what most users prefer and respond to.
- You can stitch images together—three to seven—to create a slideshow. You can display the slideshow in rectangular or square size. You can also set how long the images are visible and add in a fade from one image to the next.

Video

There are two options for video only ads: Feed videos and in-stream ads.

Feed videos appear as typical ads in a user's news feed. They are standalone, so they appear on their own. In-stream videos are similar to those you see when watching a video on YouTube. These types of ads pop up in Facebook videos that users have already seen. They do not start until at least 60 seconds of the video has been watched and only last 5 to 15 seconds. They're like little commercial breaks that cannot be skipped.

Video Feed Guidelines:

- Upload the highest-resolution possible
- Must be at least 600x315 for landscape videos or 600X60 for square videos
- Format should be .MP4 or .MOV
- File size can be up to 4GB
- Videos can be no longer than 240 minutes
- Can include video captions and sound
- Thumbnail images can not contain more than 20% text

In-Stream Video Guidelines:

- Upload the highest resolution possible
- Aspect ratio should be 16:9, this depends on the aspect ratio of the main video
- Format should be .MP4 or .MOV
- The largest file size can be 4G
- Length of videos needs to be kept between 5-15 seconds

- Captions and sounds are allowed but should again match the main video style
- Thumbnail images must not contain more than 20% text

Carousel

Carousel ads let you add multiple images, videos, or a combination of both. People seeing this type of ad can swipe through to see the different products you offer all in one place.

Image Guidelines:

- Image size must be at least 600X600, though 1080X1080 is the most preferred
- Image files must be .jpg or .png
- Images can have no more than 20% text on them
- Must have at least 2 image cards and up to 10

Video Guidelines:

- Videos should be 1080X1080 pixels
- Aspect ratio should be 1:1
- Video format should be in MP4 or .MOV
- Max size can be 4GB
- Length of video can be no longer than 240 minutes
- The thumbnail image can have no more than 20% text

Instant Experience

This is another format option where you can create a full-screen ad experience. Previously known as Canvas, Instant Experiences are great for any goal or object you choose but are only shown to mobile users. These ads let you customize your ads to give viewers instant access to information about your business, show your products or service, or prompt the viewer to fill out forms and learn more about your brand.

An instant experience ad can have several pages and you can include multiple components. Facebook provides several Instant Experience templates to create your ads. This is the best way to design an experience to ensure optimal results. The pre-designed templates are specially designed to align with your marketing goals. You can include images, videos, and text in your ads, but there are a few other components to know about as well.

Image Guidelines:

You can use up to 20 images in your Instant Experience. Images should follow these guidelines.

- Images can be formatted to fit-to-width or fit-to-height. The full width of an image should be 1080px and full height is 1920px
- Images must be in .png or .jpg formats

- Designate a cover image. This image must adhere to the same requirements of an image feed ad
- Animated images or gifs should follow video guidelines, not image guidelines

Video Guidelines:

Videos by default are set on a loop with no sound. There is no limit to how many videos you can include in your ad, but the total combined duration of the videos cannot exceed two minutes.

- Videos can be set to full-width or fit the user's screen
- The highest resolution is recommended but videos must be at least 720p
- Video format should be MP4 or .mov
- Videos should be fit for portrait aspect ratio. If your video is in landscape, it will be resized which can result in pillar boxes
- Do not use captions on your videos

When you are adding videos, you want to have just one video on each page. Having more than one video results in multiple videos playing back at the same time.

Text Guidelines:

There are several areas you can add text to. Each text block can include up to 500 words. Things to know about the text feature:

- The text will appear in the theme background color—white or dark gray
- You can use Serif or San Serif font
- Font size can be between 6-72pt
- You can change the style of text—bold, italic, underline—for the whole block but not for individual words
- Text can be center, left, or right alignment

Button Guidelines:

Instant Experience ads must contain at least one button. You can have a primary CTA button as well as secondary CTA's to give viewers more options to learn more if they are not ready to purchase or perform the primary action you would like them to take.

- Buttons can be filled with color or have a colored outline that lets the background color fill the inside space. Both of these are optional.
- Buttons must be 48px in height
- They must have 48px "padding" or space from at top and bottom

- Fonts used on text for the bottom must be Serif or Sans Serif
- Font color is optional

There is also a back button featured on the top left of the screen This is required and allows the users to close the ad and return to their news feed. The back buttons are small white arrows with a darker outline, so they stand out on the white or dark gray backgrounds.

A swipe/scroll button is also displayed on the first screen of the ad.

Tilt-to-Pan Feature

The tilt-to-pan feature is optional but gives the user a more personalized experience and will provide them with easy access to additional information. This feature lets the person tilt their phone to the left or the right to get more information about the featured image or video. You can turn this feature off by selecting the fit-to-height option. Tilt-to-pan components should meet the following recommendations:

- Images and videos can be up to 5400px, though for optimal performance they should be 3240px

- Elements are always centered on the screen but will fill 100% of the height
- You can add a CTA, but the text for the CTA must be added to the image or video
- Images are compressed to enhance performance, which can cause text to blur

When you create an Instant Experience ad, keep the following in mind:

1. You want to capture people's attention as soon as they see your ad. Since this type of ad opens up into a full-screen preview on their phones, you need to give them a reason to click on the ad to see more.

2. Showcase your company name, product name, or logo in the first layout. This will reiterate to the viewer what the ad is about, and why they initially clicked on the ad in the first place.

3. Mention the strongest points you want the viewer to remember early and often. Most viewers may not watch the entire ad, which means if you leave the best for last it may never get seen. You can highlight key points about your product or brand more than once and give multiple calls to action throughout the viewing experience. Each

screen of the Instant Experience can have its own call to action which you should take advantage of.

4. Use a mixture of elements. Do not limit your Instant Experience ads to just a photo or video with some text. Have at least five components to your ad that will keep viewers interested and eager to see more. Be sure to use high-quality images and videos.

5. Do not overcomplicate it. You can reuse material from posts or ads you have already created.

Steps for Lead Generating Ads

While not necessarily a format, there are additional steps after the creative part of the ad process that are taken when using a lead-generating ad. During this step you will find a few CTA options:

- Apply Now
- Download
- Get Quote
- Learn More
- Sign Up
- Subscribe

If you already have a lead form created, you can use that with any of the CTA buttons. You can also create a Lead From using the Facebook Lead Form customization section. Here you will name your form and set the language. Then you can choose what information you want viewers to input. Email and full name are the default setting but clicking on these options will reveal a list of nearly 20 more options to choose from.

After selecting the information that you want to gather, you have the option to add three questions for viewers to answer. There are already suggestions that focus on buyer intent, details of what they plan to buy, and an open-ended question. You type whatever question you want in these fields and you can give answer suggestions or allow the viewer to fill in their own answer.

Once your questions are set, Facebook will ask you to provide a link to your privacy policy or any legal disclaimers on your website. Then you can add the link to your website so viewers will be directed there after completing your form.

One additional item you can add to your Lead Forms are Context Cards. These let you provide a little more information about your offer or what people should do next. These are great for highlighting the benefits of filling out the lead form and further explain what you are offering. These cards include:

- A headline

- Benefit text in paragraph or bullet form
- Button text

Once you have everything completed, you want to view the flow of your lead forms. If you are satisfied with the form you can save the Lead Form to use for future ads.

Chapter 5: How to Set Up Facebook Ad Sets

Facebook ad sets are one of the most crucial steps in your marketing structure. This is where you determine your budget and identify your target marketing for each ad you will create. If you do not set up your ad sets correctly or manage them appropriately, they can be a waste of time and money.

Setting a Budget

How much should you spend on your ads? Once you have chosen the right campaign, it is time to establish your budget. You have two options for a budget: daily or lifetime. Once the budget is set you cannot change it after you have created your ad sets, so if you decide to go with a daily budget that is what you must stick with for the entire campaign. It is important to carefully consider which option is better suited for the campaign you are choosing to run. Each option is optimized based on the objective you set.

Daily Budget

A daily budget lets you set how much you want to spend on the ad per day. From this data, Facebook will decide which days you will have the greatest potential for reaching your goal and spend a little more from your daily budget; on days where there is lower potential, they will take less. Your daily spend will fluctuate throughout the week, but the total will not exceed the sum available.

For example, if you want to spend $10 a day, that gives Facebook $70 to spend that week running ads. Taking your goal, audience, and additional data into consideration, they believe on Sunday, Wednesday, and Friday you have the highest reach potential, so they might spend $15 on those days running your ad. On the remaining days, they will spend $10 or less.

With this option, you can set the starting budget, and select an unlimited duration for how long those ads will run. You can go back and change the daily budget size or pause your campaign.

Lifetime Budget

A lifetime budget is ideal if you plan on running your campaign more than once. You decide on the budget for your total campaign. Remember, each campaign can have more than one ad set, which means you are budgeting for multiple ads to be run at a designated time. Once you have your dates set, Facebook will average the amount that can be spent on each day.

Ad Bidding

When deciding on how much to set for your budget, you need to take into consideration Facebook Ad bidding. Bidding is how much you are paying to get your target audience to perform a specific action, for instance, cost per click or cost per 1000 impressions. This is connected to the objective you choose.

If the goal of your campaign is to raise brand awareness, such as getting likes or more video views, your bid will run on cost per impression. If you want to drive traffic to your website, your bid will be based on clicks to websites. You can also use bidding to increase sales or gain subscribers. To boost sales, you will need to set a Facebook pixel on your website; we will cover this in more detail in the next chapter.

Bidding can be done automatically for you or you can enter bids manually. Those who are newer to Facebook ads are recommended to go with the automatic bid until you have gained a better understanding, become familiar with average bids, and cost-per-result bids. Selecting automatic bidding lets Facebook decide how much you should be paying to get the most clicks.

Manual bids let you determine how much you pay for the desired action. If you know how much those click-throughs are worth, you will want to set your own bid. Facebook will give suggested bids and automatically insert one for you, but you can ultimately change the suggested bid. Setting bids helps you optimize your marketing strategy. You will only pay for the clicks you get until your maximum budget is reached.

Target Audience

Running effective ads relies on understanding your audience. Knowing their language, interactions, and when they are online will allow you to strategically run your ads for the biggest returns.

Buyer's Persona

Before you begin to set your target audience, you should have your ideal customer in mind. Creating an avatar or buyer persona can help you better understand how to serve your audience. This is not just important for running ads. The buyer's persona can help you with content creation as well as building services or packages that will directly appeal to those in your target audience. When creating a profile for your ideal customer, answer the following questions:

1. What products or services does your company offer? List everything including how your customer service is handled, return policies, and perks for VIP customers.

2. What can your products or services do to improve your customers' life?

3. Who are the people that would benefit from what your business offers?

4. What makes your product or service stand out from competitors?

5. What factors in the buyer's life will contribute to them deciding to buy your product or service? Where are they in their life in terms of career, family, finances, and lifestyle?

6. What is their buying process? Do they need to research, or will they buy on impulse?

Once you have answered these questions about your potential buyer, you can begin crafting a full biography about them. This should include:

- The specific products or services that will benefit your customer.
- The problem or pain points your customer is struggling with that your product or services can solve for them.
- Who needs to have the pain points resolved (working moms, young adults, those just out of college)?
- What are their hobbies, interests, and behaviors?
- What is their career or what industry do they work in?
- What can they afford to spend on your product or what can they afford to spend in general?

This persona will give you a starting point for setting your target audience. As you continue running your Facebook ads, it is important to review the data from your campaigns and gauge them against your initial ideal customer image. If the image you created does not match the data you collect, you need to reconsider who is in your actual market.

It is also a good idea to run surveys or ask your followers to participate in a survey that will let you gain more concrete data about your buyers. In exchange for participating in the survey, you can offer a special promotion or discount. Giving a small incentive is well worth getting real feedback from customers that will let you know exactly how your business can improve.

Setting Your Audiences

Once you have your buyer's persona completed, you can begin to utilize this to set your target audiences. To reach new customers that may not even know your company exists, you will want to focus your attention on targeting the demographics and interest sections. The basic demographic you can set include:

- Location
- Age
- Gender
- Language

You can narrow down these demographics to include specific interests, behaviors, and much more. There are thousands of options to choose from. This is why knowing your audience and regularly posting is vital. Your post performance can give you important details about your audience's interests and habits.

You can layer your audience targeting for the best results. This is done by setting the basic demographics for your target audience, then setting interests that relate to your campaign. Once you have set the parameters, you can layer on life events, income brackets, and other variables that will let you narrow in on the ideal customer.

If you want to reach individuals who know about your business or who have interacted with your posts or page in the past, you want to go with a custom audience approach. This will help you target your warm audience or those that already know and trust you. For a custom audience, you create an audience based on a few variables:

- Customer files. This lets you use a file of already existing followers of your page. This can also be used to upload a subscriber list or email list of people who are already interested in your business. These people may not follow you on Facebook and with this option, you can find them and target them with your ad.

- Website traffic. This lets you cater your ads to reach those who have visited your website or a site that is similar to yours. The Facebook pixel allows you to easily collect data about users' interaction with your website. You will find this custom audience option beneficial to remind those who have visited your website but may not have followed through with a purchase.

- App activity. Caters to people who use an app you provide or have done a certain task on an app that you created.

- Engagements on Facebook. Create a list of followers who engage with your page.

Lookalike Audiences

There is also a way to target lookalike audiences. This is one of the most effective ways to create an ad for finding new audience members. Facebook collects data from its algorithm and lets you enter specific data points to customize an audience that perfectly matches the users that are already following you. In simple terms, you are creating a clone of someone already engaging, (using your products or services) and telling Facebook to find more people like them. You can create a lookalike target audience in four ways:

1. Video lookalike audiences that focus on finding more people similar to the ones already fully watching the videos you create and post on your page.

2. Email list lookalikes that utilize your existing subscriber/email list to find more people similar to those already subscribing to you.

3. A conversion lookalike audience lets you use information from your existing audience that has performed conversion tasks—opting in for a discount code, visiting a specific page on your website, and making a purchase. Facebook will use data from existing followers that meet these parameters to find others with similar profiles.

4. Page likes lookalikes are constructed from the fans that you already have and actively engage on your posts.

Chapter 6: Running Facebook Ads

There are a few ways you can optimize how your ads are seen by Facebook users. Scheduling your ads and running them for the appropriate timeframe also needs to be carefully considered when you begin to run your ad. In this chapter, we will cover what you should know about running your ads, from scheduling to placement, and a few other key tools to utilize.

Running Ads

After you have set your budget and target audience, it is time to make a schedule for your ads. Along with the scheduling you also determine how to optimize your ad delivery. This gives your ads a better chance of being seen by the most people in a given time period.

Scheduling

If you opt for a lifetime budget, you can set up a custom ad delivery schedule. You decide the days and times your ad gets run. When setting up a custom schedule, the ads will run according to your time zone.

It is important to consider how long you want your ads to be shown. Running the same ad for too long can make a poor impression on users as they will get bored right away. You need to also factor in your budget when you set the duration of your ad. If your budget is too long, and you set your ad to run for weeks, you may struggle to achieve the desired results. You can always change your budget to better fit your duration. For most, successful ads will run for five days up to two weeks.

Ad Delivery

You will choose your ad delivery optimization after you set your budget in the setup process. Here you tell Facebook what your end goal is for the ad. You can choose between standard and accelerated ad delivery. With standard delivery, your ad will be shown for the lowest cost but optimal speed. Accelerated delivery will get your ads out as fast as possible which tends to be more costly. Accelerated ad delivery is better suited for time-sensitive ads where you need to have a quick turnaround by a fast-approaching date, such as an approaching sale, product launch, or event.

Ad Testing

Whether you are just starting with Facebook ads or have already run a few, ad testing is important. There are plenty of ways you can test out your ads. These tests will give you valuable information on how your ads are performing overall, and how they are performing within your target market. There are a handful of ad tests you can perform on Facebook, which give you plenty of options to gather more data.

Conversion Lift or Brand Lift

These tests, or experiments, are a great place to start in the testing process. They will give you an idea of how your advertising is impacting your conversion rates or brand awareness. Using the Facebook experiment tool, you can start a conversion lift or brand lift.

A conversion lift will show you how your Facebook marketing is impacting your defined objective. For this test, select an objective along with the campaign you want to test and create a hypothesis. Your intended audience is split into two groups. One group is intentionally shown to you, and the other is hidden. The actions taken by both groups during the duration of the test are tracked. This will allow you to see which group of people are making purchases, asking questions, or visiting your website. This information lets you calculate the impact of your advertising efforts and help reveal improvements you can make when targeting your audiences.

A brand lift helps you see how your Facebook advertising performs without taking into consideration other marketing efforts. Unlike lift tests that will show you how your conversion rates are affected, brand lifts show you how memorable and effective your ads are at creating brand awareness. These tests will show you if the message of your ads is clear, if people remember your brand or products, and if they would buy from you. These tests are only performed when you don't have any ads running at the time. This will give you a realistic view of your marketing efforts since your audience will not have a chance to see advertisements from your company. You can use the Facebook brand survey test for running campaigns or to use with all your advertisements to gather information about your brand awareness efforts.

A/B Testing

Facebook allows you to conduct A/B testing in several ways. This gives you the opportunity to change a variable in your campaign or ad set to see how they perform next to one another. You can do this by going into the Ads Manager Toolbar. If you click on the box to the left of your campaign or ad sets you want to test, you can then select the A/B test option from the top panel. From here you will see a list of variables to test:

- Creative. These are changes to the format of the ad. Use this to test out how different images perform against one another, test if video or images do better, or test out different text on ads.
- Audience. Test ads in different audiences or different demographics.
- Delivery optimization. See if ads do better with campaign budget optimization.
- Placement. Try different ad placements.
- Product set. See how product sets compete against each other.
- Custom variable. This lets you change multiple variables of your ad structure. These can be a combination of variables from the campaign, ad set, or ad level.

You can conduct A/B testing by duplicating existing ads, but this only allows you to change the creative variables. You must duplicate the campaign or use experiments to test additional variables.

Facebook Pixels and Facebook SDK

When it comes to increasing conversion rates, Facebook has made it easier than ever for a business to optimize its efforts. The Facebook pixel and Facebook SDK are designed to track different activities that will help you precisely target key audiences.

Facebook Pixel

The Facebook pixel is a unique piece of code that gets added to your website's code (you may need the assistance of a website developer to ensure this is done properly). Once added, the pixel will track actions on your site and specific pages, such as on your purchase page or add-to-cart page. When someone performs an action, the pixel is activated to record the data. The more times visitors perform the identified action, the better Facebook can optimize your ads to reach the people who are more likely to engage with your ads.

Facebook pixels are also essential for your remarketing strategy which we will cover more in the last chapter. These pixels can give you crucial data about people who visit your website, either on their own or via your Facebook ad or page. With this information you can:

- Create a custom audience for more effective targeting.
- Get insight on your website traffic.
- Learn how your ads perform across different devices.
- Target the people on Facebook who are most likely to take action on your ads.

Facebook SDK

The Facebook SDK works similarly to the Facebook pixel, except that it is used for apps instead of websites. The SDK gathers data from your app users, so you can track their activity and see what actions they are taking when they use your app. To use this feature, you will need to register your app with Facebook on the App Dashboard. The SDK automatically will capture any events where someone installs, launches, and completes a purchase through your app. You can add additional events to gather information that better aligns with your marketing goals. This is done by setting custom events.

Like the Facebook pixel, the Facebook SDK tool is essential for remarketing. Facebook will utilize this information to optimally target audiences that specifically use apps for purchases, and who will be more likely to perform a specific action request through your Facebook ads.

Ad Placement or Display

Where will your audience be able to view your ads on their desktop and mobile device? Facebook has a few options to get your ads seen by the most users, and you can customize this based on knowing what type of device your audience tends to log on with.

Right Column Ads

These used to be the standard display. This features your ad on the right column of the users' feed. These ads, however, are only visible to desktop users which is why they are not as popular as they once were. Right column ads are also smaller and have a few more restrictions in formatting. They do not contain as much information as a feed ad, and they can only contain landscape or horizontal images.

Feed Ads

These ads are shown in the news feed. They appear as a typical Facebook post which can be either beneficial or a hindrance. While news feed ads allow both desktop and mobile users to easily see your ads, it also makes it easier for them to get lost in feeds. Because they blend in with posts from others, they can easily be looked over and passed up. To reduce the risk of your ad getting brushed past you need to ensure that it is eye-catching. This is done by creating a tagline and using a high-quality image.

You can cater news feed ads to be displayed in feeds of just mobile users or those who mostly use a desktop.

Instagram Feed

You can reach more people on Instagram if you cross-promote. You can add your Instagram account to any ad set by changing the placement setting. You can also create a new campaign that will display your ads on both Instagram and Facebook. To do this, you need to link your Instagram account to your business page. Doing this also lets you share content from Instagram to your business page or story instantly.

Messenger

This option displays your ads on the home screen of Facebook messenger. On the mobile app, these will appear as a new chat message. When people go into their messenger, they will see your ad and be able to click on it just as they would a news feed ad. This is often an underused placement option but is ideal for starting conversations with your audience. This is also an ideal option when you are retargeting your ads, since this lets you reach out to individuals directly who have already shown interest in your business.

Chapter 7: Managing Your Ads

What is convenient and beneficial about Facebook marketing is it provides you with all the tools you need to track, adjust, and learn from your marketing efforts. These tools are not just to help you run a successful ad campaign, but they will also help you have a more successful business page. This chapter will go over the tools you should familiarize yourself with.

Business Management Accounts and Tools

The Facebook insight tool and audience insight tool are two features you want to use regularly. These tools will help you not only expand on your marketing efforts but ensure you do so intentionally.

Facebook Insights

Facebook insights let you track the activity on your page. These insights give you the option to quickly glance at data, view your branding efforts, and see in-depth information on the performance of your page. There are several elements of

Facebook insights that can help you stay on track with your marketing goals.

Overview shows you a glimpse of key metrics of your page.

Page summary gives you a quick view of your page's performance from the previous five days. Here you will see the likes, engagement reach, and your reach along with how these have changed from the previous week.

Most recent posts show the day you posted, a snippet of your post, the type of post, reach, (organic and paid), and engagement. The engagement is divided to show you how many clicks your post got, as well as reactions. You will also find a boost post button that lets you quickly use one of these recent posts to gain more traction if it is performing well. This section is valuable because it lets you see how your content is doing. Each of the posts are stacked on top of one another, making it easy to compare how one post is performing against another. You can use this information to create more engaging and preferred content. If you click on the post, you will see additional information and more detailed metrics. When you click on a video post, you will see how many minutes of the video was viewed, the average watch time, and how many total views the post got.

Pages to watch is great to see how your page is doing compared to similar pages. Here you will find the top five or six pages that are similar to yours and see how many likes they averaged that week compared to the previous week. It will also tell you how many posts the page has published and their engagement. If you click on any of these pages you will see their top post for the week. Utilize this information to keep track of trends and to gain knowledge about what potential competitors are already doing.

Exporting data is more in-depth data from your page insights. Facebook allows you to download a CSV or Excel spreadsheet that will show you metrics on:

- Page data which covers engagement, likes, and audience.
- Post data to see reach, impressions, and feedback.
- Video data to uncover how many unique, paid, and organic views videos received.

You can choose up to 500 posts at a time to gain further metrics. You are also able to set a date range, which lets you choose data from a specific date set.

Facebook Audience Insight

The audience insight tool will provide you with valuable information on your target audience. Data is gathered from both the people who already like and engage with your page, as well as the rest of Facebook users. Understanding and making use of these tools will let you create highly targeted ads for both groups of people, so you can find more of your ideal clients or customers. With this tool you can gather information on:

- Demographics
- Page likes
- Location
- Language
- Usage
- Purchase activity

You can further find data on special interests, life events, and lifestyles. With this information, you can find trends in your current customers and people who already like your page and look for these same trends among other Facebook users.

Gauging Ad Performance

There are a lot of factors that contribute to your ad running successfully. Knowing which of these factors needs to be adjusted or reconfigured will allow you to make necessary changes to improve your results. Facebook makes it easy for business owners to see how well their ads are performing to meet their marketing goals. The Ads Manager dashboard provides you with various tools that you should become familiar with when you begin running ads on Facebook. If you have already created a campaign, then you have already been using the Ads Manager. You can also edit your ads from here. More importantly, you can see how your ads are performing.

Account Overview

Your account overview is where you can quickly see how your ads are performing. This will give you valuable insight into how to create future campaigns and ads. Here you will find a summary of all the campaign's performances. You will also be able to view data about the demographics of the people viewing your ads. From your account overview you can:

- Spot trends or patterns through the charts provided. You can see what time of day people clicked on your ads, so you know when to time your ads going forward.

- Review data from your audience to pinpoint the region where they are more likely to click on your ad. This will allow you to create ads that cater specifically to the people in this area to increase conversion rates or strengthen brand awareness.

Additionally, creative reporting focuses on the creative aspect of your ad, such as the visuals and text elements. This reporting tool does more than just show which videos or images resonate better with your audience. You can see data on your highest and lowest performing ads based on specific creative metrics. Creative reporting shows you specific details of your ad's creative performance in several ways:

- Reporting tables show you the reach, impression, cost per result, and amount spent.

- Customized breakdowns let you see audience detail, placement, and other data based on your ad creatives. With breakdowns, you learn the age of your audience, where they tend to view your ads, what devices they favor, and other helpful information.

- Performance issues with your ad creatives.

- Engagement rate, conversion, and the quality of your ad are ranked.

- Get troubleshooting solutions to improve your ad creatives.

Campaign, Ad Sets, and Ad Data

The account overview lets you see how your ads are moving you towards your bigger marketing goals, but you can also dive deeper into how each campaign, ad set, and ad are helping or hindering these efforts. When you select Campaigns, Ad sets, or Adoption in the Ads manager, you can see in-depth reviews of various aspects of ad structure. Some of the data you can uncover here include:

- Metrics of your ad structure where you can select different metrics like reach, delivery, impression, and actions to view how your ad performed in those specific areas.

- Suggested columns provide you with additional data based on the campaign object and ad creative.

- Breakdowns let you see how the elements of your ad structure performed among target audiences. You can see data based on delivery, action, and time to know which audience is the best for what you offer. This will allow you to target these people in future ads.

Saving Reports

You can save the metrics chosen from Campaigns, Ad sets, or Ads reports to use again. This will let you easily utilize these filters with future campaigns. Another benefit of creating and saving these types of reports is that you can select a date range as well. This helps you understand what time of year your target audience is more inclined to buy. You can also send these reports to yourself or others on your management team. You will be able to access these whenever you need to quickly refer to them before you create a new ad structure.

Chapter 8: Remarketing and Retargeting

Just because you miss the mark a couple times doesn't mean your ad is faulty; you may just need to retarget or rethink how you use them. When businesses see their ad frequency decrease, most will retire that campaign and start a new one. This is a common mistake. Instead of starting a brand-new campaign, you can retarget and remarket ads to increase frequency. There are also additional ways you can use Facebook marketing to achieve your business goals.

Retargeting Campaigns

Remarketing focuses on reengaging with followers or current customers on Facebook. When you remarket, you are essentially trying to reconnect with people who already know about your business. Retargeting is based on making adjustments to certain parameters to reach a new audience that you may not have tapped into before. Retargeting can be an effective way for new products you might be launching that are geared towards a completely new audience. There are several ways you can remarket or retarget on Facebook either from your own sources or Facebook sources.

Custom Audience

Custom audiences consist of the people who are already part of your Facebook audience. Whether they have just liked your page, visited your website from a previous ad, or purchase from your regularly, it doesn't matter where they are in their buying process or how long they have been following you. This audience can also consist of your subscriber list, app users, and others that you have information on that can be uploaded to Facebook. Facebook will help you find these people and create ads specifically to engage with them. You have the option to create a custom audience from a list (such as email or subscriber list), website visitors (Facebook pixel), or app users (Facebook SDK).

From a List

Just as you would for a lookalike ad built from your existing list, you can do the same to create a custom audience. You upload your list and include as many identifiers as you can about the people on your list. The more identifiers you can include, the better Facebook can match your list to users. Facebook has made this easy for you to do by creating a template you can download, fill in, and then add. If you add your own template it must be CSC or TXT files. If you do not map out your identifiers correctly, Facebook will let you know by displaying an exclamation mark.

You want to correct these identifiers before uploading your list for a better chance of getting the right matches.

From Website Visits

Using the Facebook pixel, you can create a custom audience based on any group of people who have visited your website. This can be those who land on your homepage, who visit a specific page on your website, who have made a purchase, or just browsed. You can also create a custom audience based on those who have visited your website in the last 30 days. There are plenty of variables you can use to create a custom audience via your Facebook pixel.

From App Users

Like the Facebook pixel for your website, the Facebook SDK is specifically designed for businesses that offer an app for download so customers can make purchases and stay up to date on products and services. This helps you track app user activity. This can then be used to create a custom audience. Like the pixel, you can customize the audience via the SDK data by those who have downloaded your app, placed items in a cart but have not purchased, what type of device they use (Android, or iOS), and more.

Once you have created your custom audiences, you can begin to remarket for specific purposes. Before you begin you want to ensure that you revisit your Facebook marketing goals. Remarketing on Facebook should be done only when you have a substantial following list or have a decent subscriber list. These campaigns speak directly to people on Facebook who are already aware of your brand. Remarketing helps you move your fans along in the buying process and towards becoming a loyal customer. These ads help you guide users to shop and purchase items from your business, shop again at your store, or take advantage of special deals for VIP customers.

Remarketing Strategies

When you are remarketing, it is essential that you keep three important factors in mind:

1. Your audience. After you have been running a few ads and have built up a decent group of followers, you should have a better picture of who your audience is. You may have first started out thinking you would target one group only to find another has stepped up and become loyal fans. These are the people you want to continue to build a relationship with. Listen to what your followers are saying

and then create a strategy that gives them what they want. This will help you find more people like them that will love your brand as well.

2. Always add value. Instead of focusing on how many people you can reach with your ads, think of the best ways to add the most value to people. When you add value, you will be rewarded ten-fold. People don't want to just buy from an ad, they want to buy from a brand that is relatable and solves a problem.

3. Revisit your goals. It can be easy to get caught up in evaluating data from ad performance, making adjustments to increase engagement, and all the other things to keep your Facebook page relevant. In doing this you can quickly lose sight of what you first wanted to accomplish. Before you start remarketing or building new campaigns, review your goals. Ask if these goals are still relevant or if you have gotten off course with what you initially set out to do.

Use Dynamic Ads

Facebook dynamic ads are one of the most effective ways you can retarget audience members who have been to your websites. These ads show products that they may have abandoned in their cart, viewed on a specific page from your website, or recommendations that appeal to them based on their interests.

What is even better about these ads is that they automatically work for you. You upload your product catalog, set up a campaign, and Facebook will find the right people who would be interested in each item you uploaded. It even finds new people to show products to that may have never visited your site before.

Dynamic ads utilize the Facebook pixel or Facebook SDK. If you have an online shop through Shopify, Magento, or BigCommerce, you can automatically set up dynamic ads for your shop without having to upload a catalog. Dynamic ads can appear on feeds, messenger, or Instagram to reach even more people.

Sponsored Messages

A sponsored message utilizes the messenger feature to re-engage with people you have had conversations with. This also includes those who have used the live chat support feature. Sponsored messages let you restart conversations with people, remind them of products they might be interested in, give them promotion offers, or update them about products or business information.

Sponsored ads will retarget people you have had a conversation with within the last year. They need to run for at least five days for optimal results. These ads will not be shown to people who you have just started a conversation with you in messenger though; the conversation must be at least a day old.

Additional Ways to Use Facebook Marketing

There are a few lesser-known ways you can expand your marketing on Facebook. When you have gained a clear understanding of how to utilize the traditional format, consider this additional ways you can increase brand awareness and sales.

Story Ads

Story ads are displayed in between Facebook stories. These ads can be images, videos, or a combination of the two.

Image Guidelines:

- Standalone images are only shown for five seconds
- Image size should be 1080X1920
- The image ratio should be 1:91 to 9:16
- Text should not exceed 20% of the image and should be kept within 1080X1420 of the frame.
- Image can be either .jpg or .png

Video Guidelines:

- Videos can be up to 15 seconds long
- You should always upload the highest resolution possible
- The aspect ratio should be between 1.91 and 9:16
- The maximum file size is 4GB
- Videos can be no longer than 15 seconds.
- File formats you can use include MP4 or .MOV
- Keep text and logos 250 pixels from the top and bottom of the frame.

Be sure to leave space at the top and bottom of your ad (both video and images). This is where profile images are shown, and CTA buttons are placed.

You can also change the ad placement so that they are seen on Instagram stories as well if you have an account linked to your business page.

Facebook Marketplace

You may be aware of different Facebook Marketplaces. These are communities where people can sell and buy items from other users. While many of these serve as an online garage sale or flea market of sorts, they can be a gem for businesses to find new customers. Users visit the Facebook Marketplace with the intention of buying so they are already ahead in the buying process compared with others browsing the app.

You can always create a post on the Marketplace to sell but creating an ad can get you more attention and make your efforts more successful. This is a great option for those who want to expand their local reach. Most users go to the Marketplace to find items listed by locals. The guidelines for these types of ads, for images or videos, are the same as standard feed ads.

Facebook Collection Ads

These ads are specially designed for mobile users. They are set up as a mini product catalog that features a video or image with smaller images displayed below it. The images and videos are displayed on a grid layout with a few different options:

- Storefront
- LookBook
- Customer acquisition
- Storytelling

Guidelines for Collection Images:

- Size must be 600X600
- Image ratio must be 1:1 or 9:16

- File format must be .jpg or .png
- File size can not exceed 30M
- Text can fill no more than 20% of the image

Guidelines for Collection Videos:

- Videos must be at least 1200X628
- Files can be MP4 or .MOV format
- File size can be no larger than 4GB
- Videos cannot be longer than 120
- Thumbnail image but not have more than 20% text

Conclusion

Facebook is a robust platform that allows a business to excel in many areas. Whether your goal is to increase brand awareness, expand your market, or increase traffic or sales, you can accomplish this and more through Facebook. Many businesses fail to flourish on Facebook because their approach is off. When you embrace the social aspects and utilize this to engage with people, you will see success.

You have learned there is more you can do with your Facebook page then just push out ads. Do not get overwhelmed by all the things you think you have to do right away. Creating an effective Facebook marketing plan comes down to just three core components:

1. Have a clear goal written out.
2. Consistently publish relevant and valuable posts.
3. Be open and willing to listen to your audience.

This book has provided you with all the tips and tools you need to master these three components. Now you just have to put them into action. By taking the first steps and focusing on your content, you will learn how to create highly successful ads with little to no effort.

One last bit of advice. Facebook is always changing and expanding, and it is important to stay up to date with these changes. Make it a point to keep yourself informed of any changes and additions to their ad policies. They also provide tons of useful information, tips, and best practice advice through the Facebook for business website.

Facebook marketing does not have to be complex, and you do not have to overthink it. When you shift your focus from simply gaining more customers to helping and adding value to them, you will see a higher return on your efforts. Now that you know how to be successful on Facebook, it is time to make that a reality. Thank you, and good luck!

www.ingramcontent.com/pod-product-compliance
Lightning Source LLC
LaVergne TN
LVHW011736060526
838200LV00051B/3198